Numbers At Play

A Counting Book

Numbers At Play

A Counting Book

Charles Sullivan

RIZZOLI
NEW YORK

The House Builders *by Walter Osborne, late nineteenth century*

1

Counting can be

so much fun!

And it's easy

when you begin with one!

Start with a cat

that's black and white.

How many? One?

Yes, you're right!

Walter Osborne (1859–1903). Irish artist whose charming portraits and impressionist landscapes are displayed in the National Gallery of Ireland, the Tate Gallery, and other major museums.

Find number 1

You must find the number one

to put a penny in the slot

and see which candy ball you've got.

Wayne Thiebaud (Born 1920). American artist whose work in cartoons and advertising has evolved into a distinguished career as a painter and teacher with a fresh approach to everyday objects.

Jawbreaker Machine *by Wayne Thiebaud, 1963*

Los Angeles boy learning baseball skills from Dodgers' manager Tommy Lasorda, photograph by Caryn Levy, 1990

2

How many players
wearing blue?
Start with one
and count to two.

Caryn Levy (Born 1961). American photographer, based in Miami but often traveling to distant locations. Her credits include four covers and many featured pictures for Sports Illustrated.

Find number 2

Here you have two chances
to find the number two,
the upper or the lower—
which number's best for you?

Robert Indiana (Born 1928). Artist who calls himself an "American painter of signs" because he has frequently used the stenciled numbers and letters, colors and shapes found in commercial art.

Two *by Robert Indiana,*
1960–62

Breton Girls Dancing, Pont Aven *by Paul Gauguin, 1888*

3

How many girls can you see

dancing in France?

The answer is three.

Paul Gauguin (1848–1903). Parisian artist who moved to Brittany and later to the South Pacific in search of the "unspoiled" life, which he depicted in colorful and powerful paintings.

Find number 3

Start at the top
and follow me
down the steps
to number three.

Giacomo Balla (1871–1958). Italian artist who played a large part in the abstract Futurist movement before returning to a more realistic style.

Numbers in Love *by Giacomo Balla, c. 1920*

Children on the Seashore, Guernsey *by Pierre Auguste Renoir*

4

How many children
playing on the shore?
Start with one
who loves the sun,
and count to four.

Pierre Auguste Renoir (1841–1919). Joie de vivre, a joyful attitude toward life, is reflected in this French artist's warm, tender paintings of children and adults.

London Bus II *by Red Grooms, 1983*

Find number 4

Look near the window,

look near the door—

and in between

is the number four.

5

The girl looks like a statue,
the statues seem alive—
start with number one now,
and count right up to five.

Dennis Brack (Born 1939). Born in Texas, this photographer focuses on the Washington scene, especially the lives and travels of the Presidents, but his pictures cover many aspects of life in America.

National Gallery of Art, *photograph of George Segal's* The Dancers *by Dennis Brack, 1990*

Find number 5

Find a number five that's big,

another five that's small,

and then go back and look again—

is that all?

Charles Demuth (1883–1935). American artist who developed a "precisionist" style. I Saw the Figure 5 in Gold *was inspired by the poetry of William Carlos Williams.*

I Saw the Figure 5 in Gold by Charles Demuth, 1928

Untitled *(soapbox racing) by William Henry Johnson, 1939–40*

6

How many children

want to drive this cart?

Six is the answer,

but one is where you start.

William Henry Johnson (1901–1970). African-American artist who lived in Europe for many years before returning to New York with a vision of home and heritage which he expressed in lively, powerful paintings.

Find number 6

You can do magic,

you can do tricks,

you can find

the number six.

Owh! in San Paõ *by Stuart Davis, 1951*

7

"How many children?"
asked the March Hare.
Try to count seven
playing there.

Laurie Watters (Born 1959). American photo-grapher who has spent years documenting Central Park in New York City. She particularly likes to photograph people.

José de Creeft's Alice in Wonderland, *photograph by Laurie Watters, 1991*

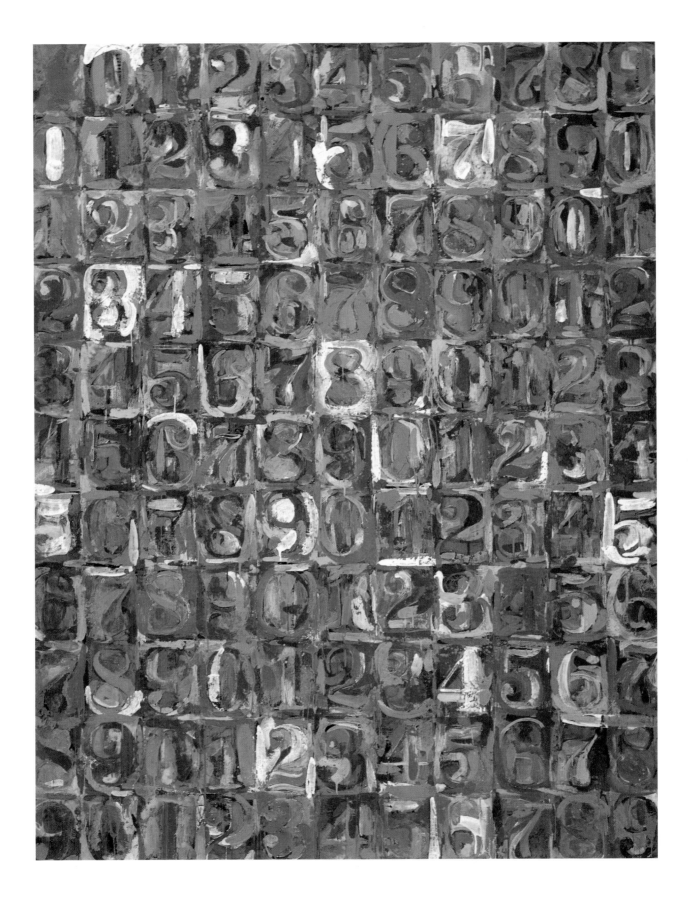

Numbers in Color *by Jasper Johns, 1958–59*

Find number 7

You'll find many numbers here,

but where does number seven appear?

Jasper Johns (Born 1930). One of the first Pop artists in America, he painted everyday objects such as numbers, flags, targets, and maps in unusual ways before moving on to more abstract compositions.

8

See them swinging
like a gate—
start with one
and count to eight.

*Winslow Homer (1836–1910). American
artist whose pictures of children—at play,
at school, at home—give us a colorful and
detailed record of life in the nineteenth
century.*

Snap the Whip *by Winslow Homer, 1872*

Painting No. 48, Berlin *by Marsden Hartley, 1913*

Find number 8

When you find it,
please don't wait—
put your thumb
on number eight.

9

Colors make
these people shine—
start with one
and count to nine.

*Fernand Léger (1881–1955). French artist
whose abstract scenes of people and buildings
are happier and more animated than those
of many of his contemporaries.*

The Great Parade *by Fernand Léger, 1954*

9 West 57th Street by Margaret Graham Kranking, 1988

Find number 9

Wouldn't it be fine,

wouldn't it be neat,

to find a number nine

just standing in the street?

Margaret Graham Kranking (Born 1930). This American painter often uses watercolors to capture the complex patterns of light and shadow in landscapes, seascapes, and interior scenes.

Ten men riding the 1896 Orient "Oriten" bicycle, photograph late nineteenth century

10

This bike can carry
how many men?
Start with one
and count to ten.

Find number 10

Everyone understands

in soccer you don't use your hands,

so in this game I suppose

you should touch number ten with your toes!

Kevin Haggard (Born 1971). A finance major at Georgetown University, he enjoys taking sports photographs for The Hoya, *a student newspaper.*

Author's Note

Counting seems difficult at first—there are so many different things to count, and so many different numbers. But the first ten numbers are usually the hardest. Later, as we move on to 11, 12, 13, and so on, we suddenly realize that our old friends 1, 2, 3, etc., are repeating themselves over and over. Soon we are racing through the twenties, thirties, forties, fifties, and so on, into the hundreds and beyond. It's like learning to ride a bicycle, then riding faster and faster, farther and farther, for the sheer fun of it!

But we have to start at the beginning and learn the basics before we can go fast, so this book concentrates on the numbers one through ten. For each of these numbers there are two presentations. The first asks the reader to count something (one cat, two baseball players, three girls dancing, four children playing on the seashore). These countable things are presented in striking pictures by Paul Gauguin, Pierre Auguste Renoir, William Henry Johnson, Winslow Homer, and other interesting artists and photographers. I have written poems explaining what to count in each picture.

The second presentation teaches the reader how to recognize each of the numbers, one through ten, again using a picture accompanied by an explanatory poem. Here we find the numeral 1 on a gumball machine painted by Wayne Thiebaud, 2 on a creation of Robert Indiana's, 3 in an abstract painting by Giacomo Balla, 4 on a London bus as only Red Grooms could depict it, and so on.

I have been very pleased to hear from readers of my earlier book, *Alphabet Animals*, and I would like to get letters from the readers of this book too. Do you like *Numbers at Play*, what do you like best, is there anything about it that you don't like? Please write and tell me what you think (my address is: Post Office Box 1775, Annapolis, MD 21404).

I dedicate this book to my grandsons, Frank Hanafee Sullivan and Edward Louis Sullivan. Hello to new readers, including Sophie Emmerson and Maxwell Freeborn. And I send a special note of thanks to my editor, Lois Brown.

Charles Sullivan
Washington, D.C.

Title page illustration:
Ten men riding the 1896 Orient "Oriten" bicycle. Photo-
graph. From the collections of Henry Ford Museum &
Greenfield Village, Dearborn, Michigan.

First published in the United States of America
in 1992 by Rizzoli International Publications, Inc.
300 Park Avenue South, New York, N.Y. 10010

Library of Congress Cataloging-in-Publication Data

Sullivan, Charles, 1933–
    Numbers at play / Charles Sullivan
        p.   cm.
    Summary: Combines counting with poetry, fine
art, and photography.
    ISBN 0-8478-1501-3
    1. Counting—Juvenile literature. 2. Number
concept—Juvenile literature. [1. Counting.] I. Title.
QA113.S9   1992
513.2'11—dc20
[E]   91-33154
                                                  CIP
                                                   AC

Designer: Pamela Fogg
Design Assistant: Betty Lew
Printed in Singapore